Martha's Menagerie

Wonderfully Wild on Martha's Farm

Photos and Text by

Martha Philbeck

<goldenpaws@embarqmail.com>

www.homeofthegoldenpaws.com
Edited & Cover by Pradeep Maheshwari
(s164gk1@Yahoo.com)

Born and raised on a farm, I grew up with a variety of animals and babies to raise. Life is a constant learning experience and it is up to us to protect and care for animals. Over the years I have had the privilege to learn a variety of things and skills that will be lost if I don't document them. This book is an effort to preserve it all for the generations to come. All the stories here are of birds and butterflies we have raised.

Chickens

We bring in the unclean eggs. You don't want to wash them because an egg is porous and the dirt will get in the pores and then the egg will die and not hatch. It breathes through the egg shell.

These have just hatched and are very wet.

It takes 21 days of keeping them in the incubator at 100 degrees to hatch. You have to roll the eggs at least twice a day to keep the yolk in the center. If not the babies will attach to the shell wall and not grow right. When they hatch they need to be kept in the incubator for 24 hours to get their strength.

They need to dry off. After they dry they will be fluffy. Then I put some feed and water in the incubator to get them started to eat.

Here they are starting to eat. You can see more chicken eggs and the small ones are quail eggs that have not hatched.

These chickens are 2 weeks old and starting to get their feathers on their wings. The bird on the left is a baby turkey.

This is a picture of a proud mother. Farmers have boxes similar to this for their chickens to lay eggs in. They put straw in the box so the eggs stay clean. A female chicken is called a hen. A young female chicken that has not laid   eggs or is just starting to is called a pullet.

This is a picture of a shelter for chickens being raised on grass. This is a picture of a rooster which is what a male chicken is called.

Once in a while you may have a bird hatch that has spraddle legs. This can be caused by uneven or too low heat in the incubator or the egg not being turned often enough. If not corrected they will die as they cannot walk to get to the feed.

One way of correcting this is to take a Band-Aid and cut it in half lengthwise. The pad in the middle will be just the right length to separate the legs. Then wrap each side of the Band-Aid around a leg, being careful to not do it too tight. It can cut off circulation if you do.

You may have to replace the Band-Aid several times if it comes loose. This will strengthen the bird's legs and within several days they will be able to walk and stand. If they have curled toes which can happen by being cramped in the shell and taking too long to get out you can bend a pipe cleaner and tape their toes to it. You can also cut out an outline of a foot on cardboard and tape the foot to it. The first night we put the Band-Aid on, it could still not stand up; I had to keep making it stand it on its feet. It was able to stand the next day, but tried to run. The next day it was walking and you could tell its legs were stronger. The following day we took the Band-Aid off.

The Butterfly and Dixie

It was the first time she had seen a butterfly. She was lying at my feet when all of a sudden she saw it. She tried to get as close as she could to get a good look.

She could not figure out what it was doing. Usually we turn them loose, but the weather had turned cold over night so we had to wait until it warmed up. Dixie looked at it from different positions.

She tried pawing at the glass. This scared the butterfly so it tried to fly away. Then she tried to lick the glass. It had never seen a tongue so big.

The monarch decided there was no danger from Dixie so it went back to its watermelon. We were told that we could give them watermelon if we were not able to turn them loose right away. They cannot fly if it is too cold. This was the last one that we hatched in 2015. The other cocoons did not hatch and we don't know if they were in a weaker state since fall was fast approaching. They would not have had time to migrate. Nature takes care of its own, we just try to help. They can fly a hundred miles a day. It takes 3 generations of butterflies to reach the end of their migration. Each generation flies about 1,000 miles in its lifetime.

The life cycle of the Monarch

The Monarch Butterfly

Change is hard at first

They only eat Milkweed. They shed their skin several times as they are growing. They start out as a white dot on a milkweed leaf. That is the egg laid by a Monarch. It is no bigger than a pin head. The egg stage lasts 4 days. It will take about a month to turn into a butterfly.

I brought in several leaves this year that had what I thought might be an egg.

I wrapped the bottom of the stem in a wet paper towel and put them in a plastic container with a lid on it. Several days later I checked and to my surprise there was a small worm about 1/4th inch long.

You can see here how small he was when I found him compared to the much larger worm.

They are messy in the middle.

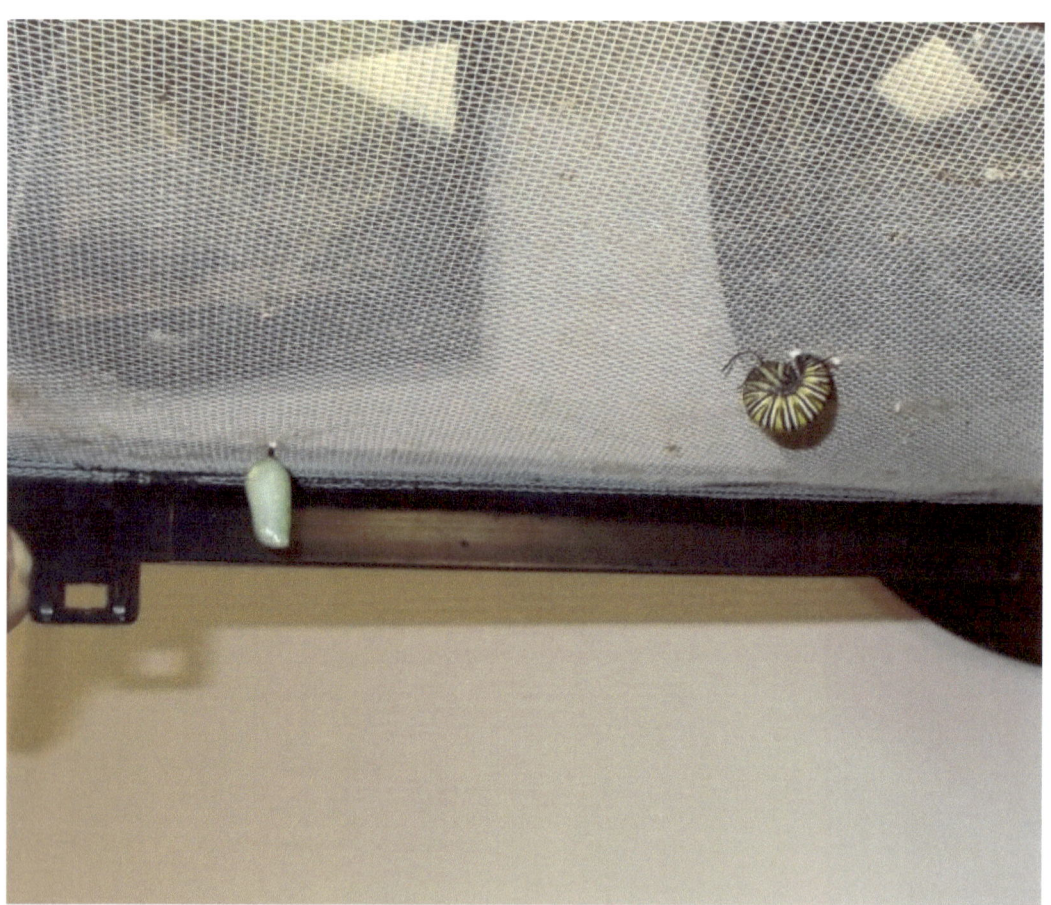

Here he is making the white silken threads that attach him to the screen. They spin a silk button to attach to the screen. You can see it in some of the photos.

Then they hang in a "J" form until they start to shed their skin.

There are several in the J form, 2 chrysalises and one that has already hatched. Notice the white dots which are the silk threads holding them to the top.

The skin splits up the back all the way to the top.

Here the skin is all the way to the top. Then he gave a big shake and it fell to the bottom of the cage. They do an exotic twisting dance to move it up.

This one has just gone into a chrysalis on a leaf. It had gotten out of the aquarium and attached to the bottom of a rocking chair and I tried to put it back. It stayed on the leaf and shed its skin as it went into the chrysalis. The skin is lying in front of it.

I tried to pick up the leaf thinking it was attached and it rolled off and broke. They dissolve into a liquid where it changes completely.

Quail

The goose

They line their nest with soft feathers from their belly. This helps to keep the eggs warm.

It takes them several days to make the nest. They will come back to the same area every year. The male stands proud and tall as he keeps watch.

You can see the crack in the egg where it is starting to hatch. Both parents take a part in raising the goslings as they are called. It takes 28 days for them to hatch.

I am getting too close and he is letting me know it.

The first thing they do is get them in the water; one parent is always on each side of the babies.

They graze on the grass as their parents stand guard. One parent is in front and one is behind. They are very protective of their babies.

They grow fast and you can already see the change in color. At this age they do not get far from the water.

He speaks softly to me as I get too close. I had raised this pair last year when the nest was destroyed and they have came back to raise their babies.

As the babies grow they change color. Look at how big their feet are. Soon they will be taking on the color of their parents.

This baby had his leg broken crossing the road and he got hit by a car. His parents wanted nothing to do with him since he was injured. I put him in a cage with food and water. Within 2 weeks he could walk again so I turned him loose in the barn with a board across the door. He jumped over the board and went back to his parents who welcomed him. I could always tell who he was by the limp he had.

Here is one learning to fly. They run really fast until their feet leave the ground.

Turkeys

This is our family of turkeys. They are not good at sitting on their eggs and hatching so I bring the eggs in and put them in an incubator.

It takes 28 days to hatch at a temperature of 100 degrees F. The eggs have to be turned twice a day to keep the baby growing in the middle of the egg.

This one has hatched quite recently.

This shows the variety of eggs in the incubator.

The big speckled egg in the center is a turkey egg. The tiny eggs are quail eggs and the other eggs are chicken eggs.

This photo is if one when it was about a week old. When they hatch notice how big the feet are. Here it is starting to grow into its feet.

These are turkeys about half grown.

When they are grown they like to strut if they are a male. They can puff themselves up.

The hens cannot make themselves look big. Notice how red the male turkeys head gets and the bristles on his chest are called a beard. A male turkey is called a tom or jake and the female is a hen.

This is a beautiful picture showing the colors of a male turkey.

Notice the stiff straight black beard on his chest and the iridescent colors of his feathers. Below is a hen with her baby. For protection against predators they get them as high as they can to sleep.

Let me end with a short note:

The 4 wheeler shatters the silence as we head out in the early morning. I am always awed by the beauty of nature. The fog is slowly lifting from the field. There is an ethereal beauty of the fog as it slowly lifts.

Lacy green fern swirl at my feet as I walk toward the sound of water gurgling over the rocks as it travels downstream. In the distance is the sound of a dog. As I listen he comes closer, he is on the trail of something. He gets excited and howls that he is on the trail of something. He is running back and forth getting closer. He jumps into the water making loud splashing noises.

He comes out into the clearing where I sit. Slowly he inches towards me as I talk to him. He looks like a black, tan and white fox hound that is in paintings of red coated riders on horses doing fox hunting. He lets me pet him and then he takes off again.

Being in the woods ties us to our roots. Trees are the guardians of our history. They have a quiet power and arresting beauty. Everyday there is something new to see. A red tailed hawk can be heard overhead as it floats above the trees searching for food.

Moonbeams kiss the tree tops at night as the fireflies light the fields and fairies sprinkle them with star dust through the night. Their wings are like netting when the moonbeams bounce off of them. They shimmer and glow as they dance from flower to flower

Her name is Twinkle Toes. She was the fastest of all the fairies. She was very tiny with hair the color of gold. She could fit in the seed pod of a milk weed using the soft down for a bed. The pod was light and could float down the stream rocking back and forth.

A quail hatching

These pictures show how a baby bird hatches out of the egg. You can see the tiny hole just starting to appear in the egg on the right. It takes 18 days at 100 degrees to hatch.

Other books by Martha.

This is the story in easy steps of the life and family and birth and nurturing of the Canadian goose. In easy to understand language you learn about the habits and needs of the Canadian goose and how to raise the young. Full knowledge about the eggs and their incubation is also included.

THE CANADIAN GOOSE
BY MARTHA PHILBECK

Hey Grandma
there's a Bird in this Egg

By Martha Philbeck

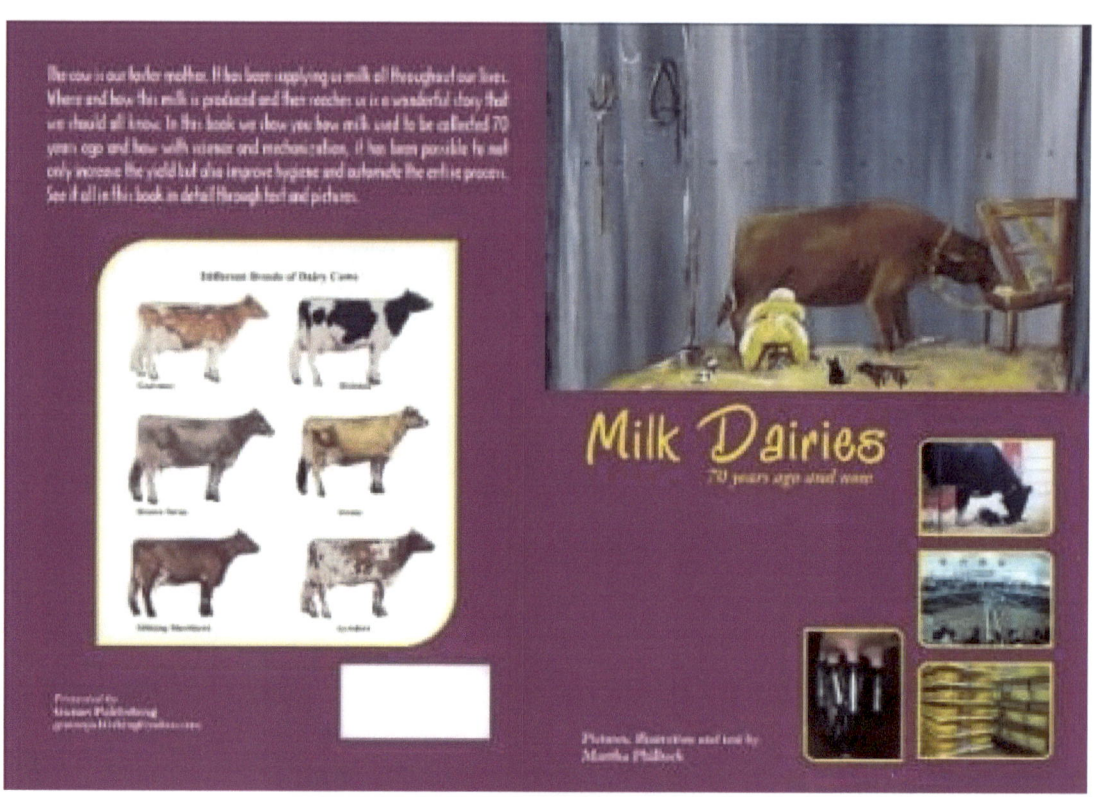

The cow is our foster mother. It has been supplying us milk all throughout our lives. Where and how this milk is produced and then reaches us is a wonderful story that we should all know. In this book we show you how milk used to be collected 70 years ago and how with science and mechanization, it has been possible to not only increase the yield but also improve hygiene and automate the entire process. See it all in this book in detail through text and pictures.

Different Breeds of Dairy Cows

Presented by
Grainert Publishing

Milk Dairies
70 years ago and now

Pictures, illustration and text by
Martha Philbeck

WILDLIFE ON MARTHA's FARM

The farm is a place of solace where we can connect with nature and vibrant life.

Pictures and texts by Martha Philbeck.

48

THE GOLDEN BOOK OF
GOLDEN RETRIEVERS

A compendium of their history, history and training

By Martha Philbeck

A lovely story of a goose that found it difficult to take off but did not give up. By sheer dint of will power and application he did finally manage to fly of course, with the help of his father!

The Goose that could not Fly

Promoted by:
Ganas Publishing
ganaspublishing@yahoo.com

USA

By Martha Philbeck

Poignant stories by children and for children; an interesting and heart rending collection.

Charlie Coyote and other stories
Volume 2

Promoted by Gunas Publishing
gunaspublishing@yahoo.com

By Martha Philbeck

Isha and the Donkey

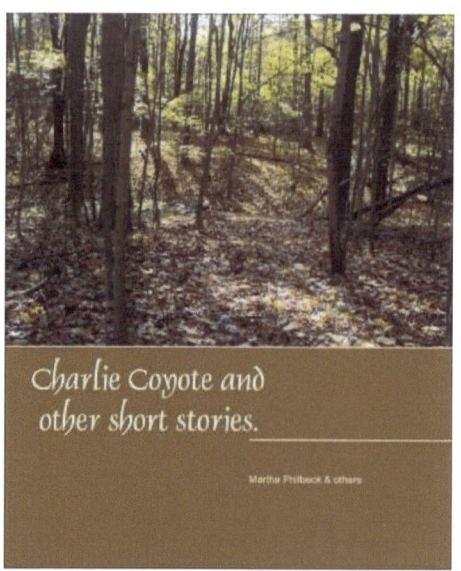

Charlie Coyote and
other short stories.

Martha Philbeck & others

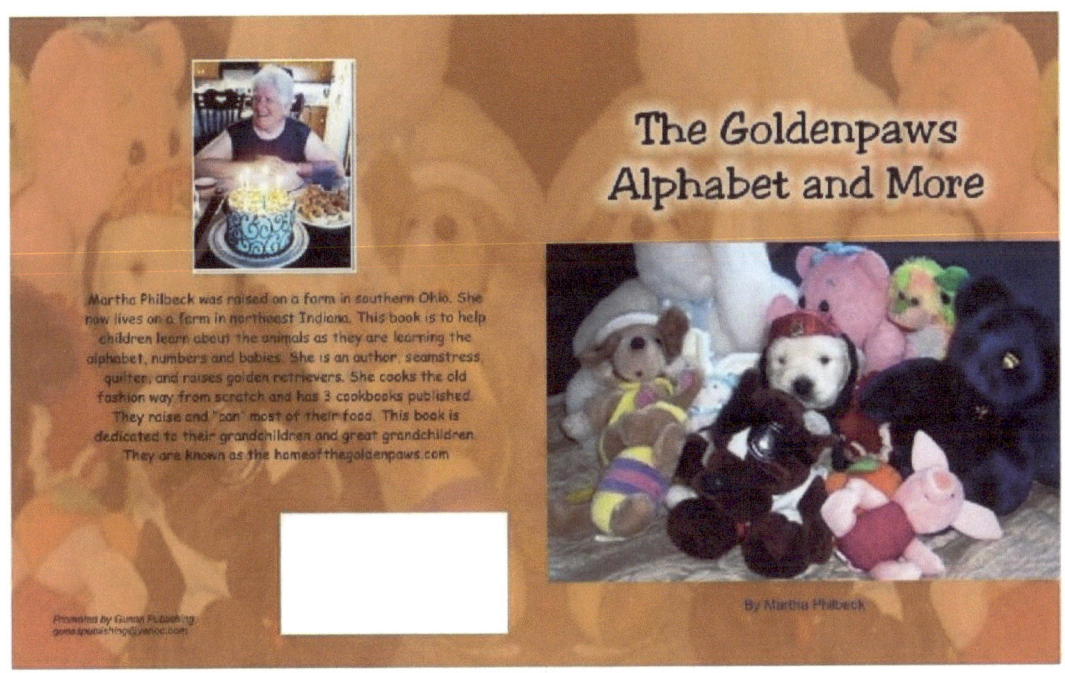

The Goldenpaws
Alphabet and More

Martha Philbeck was raised on a farm in southern Ohio. She now lives on a farm in northeast Indiana. This book is to help children learn about the animals as they are learning the alphabet, numbers and babies. She is an author, seamstress, quilter, and raises golden retrievers. She cooks the old fashion way from scratch and has 3 cookbooks published. They raise and "can" most of their food. This book is dedicated to their grandchildren and great grandchildren. They are known as the homeofthegoldenpaws.com

By Martha Philbeck

Promoted by Guma Publishing,
guma.tpublishing@yahoo.com

by Martha Philbeck

Martha Philbeck
HOME OF THE GOLDENPAWS
www.homeofthegoldenpaws.com

www.ingramcontent.com/pod-product-compliance
Lightning Source LLC
Chambersburg PA
CBHW041510280526
45792CB00004B/1203